The Luminous Cloud

THE LUMINOUS CLOUD

A series of Devotional Studies in
verse and prose set in the context
of a visit to Indian Leprosy Centres

by

Walter Fancutt

With good wishes,
Walter Fancutt

Published by
ARTHUR JAMES LIMITED
THE DRIFT EVESHAM WORCS.
WR11 4NW

First Edition 1980

©*Walter Fancutt 1980*

All rights reserved by the publishers
Arthur James Limited of Evesham, Worcs., Eng.

Fancutt, Walter
The luminous cloud
1. Christian life
I. Title
248   BV4501.2
ISBN O-85305-221-2

Printed by Gibbons Barford Print, Wolverhampton

FOREWORD

SOME PEOPLE go through life with eyes fast shut and with minds hermetically sealed. They fail to notice the exciting and significant events that are happening around them every day, and they fail to hear — because they do not listen — the lessons that God wants to teach them.

Mr Fancutt kept his eyes and ears wide open when he visited The Leprosy Mission's Centres in India. He noticed and he reflected. In this book he shares with us some of his moving experiences, etched with percipience and deep sensitivity. In relating these experiences to a rich knowledge of the Scriptures, he sheds new light on familiar passages.

There is pathos here, and courage; the dark clouds of suffering are shot through with the light of faith. These quiet meditations will bring comfort and challenge to all who have eyes to see and hearts to respond. The author's accompanying verses add the dimensions of depth of feeling and sublime exploration of spiritual truth to the prose commentary.

I wish this little book a wide and discerning public.

Stanley G. Browne.

DEDICATION

To Stanley and Mali Browne whose life and work have brought untold comfort and hope to the leprosy sufferers of the world.

THE WORD OF FORGIVENESS

"Father Forgive!" — *Luke 23:34*

Sublime apotheosis, selfless love
Which in the hour of agony and pain
Can thus forget torn flesh and reeling brain;
By one short word take wing to realms above,
And in the next reprieve the hate that drove
The spikes through hands and feet, while hearts
that feign
Thy Father's will, make mock of Thine own reign
With slender reed, and sprig of thorn inwove.
Once more Golgotha's road is stained with blood
And dark the sky, pierced only by the moan
Of tortured souls who sink beneath the cross.
Teach us afresh the mystic Fatherhood
And if, in mercy, Thou wilt not disown
Thy race, grant us redemption in our loss.

1

THE LUMINOUS CLOUD

IF I WERE ASKED to suggest a fitting symbol for sickness I would have no hesitation in complying. I would draw a dark cloud hanging low over the head of a man as he seeks to go on his way; a cloud that blots out the light of the sun, even though it cannot stop the sun from shining; a cloud that compresses the air currents with its leaden weight, encouraging the thunder and lightning as an accompaniment to the storm which it heralds.

There is an immediacy about a dark cloud which depresses because it hides so much that adds beauty to the earth, making us insensitive to the fact that we see only one side — the darker side at that — and this can impair belief in the sunlight beyond the cloud. I remember struggling across a common on the eastern edge of London, engulfed in an acrid green fog, and quoting to myself Charles Kingsley's lines:

"Dear child, I have no song to sing you:
No lark could pipe in skies so dull and grey."

Suddenly, as if in rebuke, I heard the sweet, liquid warbling of a lark, singing above the fog. Around me all was gloomy and the green grass, leafy branches and blossoming shrubs were hidden in the temporary, black-out of the fog. Yet, only a little distance above my head the sun was shining and the lark had been able to pierce the fog with its tiny wings and was singing to match the sunshine; the cloud was luminous!

It is only to be expected that there will be grey days when it is far from easy to accept the disciplines which life imposes. When the gloom has its foundation in physical weakness and chronic illness, the spirit of depression is easy to understand and difficult to move. Yet, in leprosy centres all over the world, there is evidence of a spirit far from depressing, and those of us who pass through times of low-spirit can learn much from the experience of those "whose hearts grow weary with heavier woe."

An old mystic left behind a valuable prescription, which many of our leprosy workers would confirm, when he wrote: "The adversaries of gloom are the singing of psalms and the labour of the hands, but that which kills it outright is prayer." Here, then, is the threefold cure for care: praise, service and prayer, taken in regular doses, become the antidote for

> "The slings and arrows of outrageous fortune,
> The heart-ache, and the thousand natural shocks
> That flesh is heir to."

Certainly, praise, service and prayer are never absent from the daily routine of the hospitals I visited on a tour of Indian leprosy centres. The day begins with prayers in the office, hospital ward, or clinic waiting room; prayer which goes far beyond the life of the patients and staff themselves, reaching out to the four corners of the earth in fervent intercession. The note of praise includes not only the hymns, sung with such vigour, but also the joy of life expressed in music and laughter. The critic might easily ask "What have they to sing about?" as he learns of their condition and hears their stories, but such a superficial view overlooks the indomitable spirit of man which overcomes obstacles because they are there to be vanquished.

My lark refused to be conditioned by the fog and soared to a brighter region and "could scarce get out his notes for joy." On one occasion, an Indian doctor and I were walking through the compound at Purulia in West Bengal and instinctively we stopped in our tracks, captivated by music coming on the evening air. We followed the sound of music and came to a little clearing in front of the men's quarters. The men patients were squatting on their haunches, listening to a group of patients playing a selection of folk-tunes. A hand organ, harmonica, drums and wooden clappers formed the ensemble; and when we left, a few hours later, the music was still filling the air with melody. The anguish of life had been dispelled for a while by the joyous note of praise.

Among the children who sang for me at Vadathorasalur in South India, were two young brothers Athimoolam and Marimuthoo but I am sure the two little boys would not have had a song for me if I had come across them a year or so before, when they were begging in the bazaar of a town twenty-five miles away. Athimoolam was eight and Marimuthoo was five when they set out for the begging line. Their parents had died; and instead of taking care of them the adult relatives had promptly turned them out of their village, having seen the tell-tale patches of leprosy on the skin of the boys. Hand in hand the frightened boys went out to find what shelter they could, living on what they could beg in the market, or find in the fields.

One day, as they joined the crowd of beggars making their way to a town where there was to be a religious festival, they overheard conversations about a man, reduced to begging because of leprosy, who had been away for a few years and had now returned to his village with a certificate, declaring that his leprosy was cleared and that he might return to normal employment on the home farm. At first, the headman was convinced that the certificate was a trick, perpetrated by those who no longer wished to provide for him, but both the government Collector and a local doctor upheld the certificate as genuine, so the ex-leprosy sufferer was now installed in his old home and was able to do his old job.

"Surely," said an old and crippled beggar, "if such things can happen to a man it should be possible for children to be made well; and you have nothing to lose, for you are young and in another district you can always continue your begging."

Athimoolam and Marimuthoo had never been far from their own village and its nearest town, so it was with a feeling of foreboding that they set out for Vadathorasalur, their only clue being a scrap of paper on which someone had written the name of the place. Little Marimuthoo's legs soon tired but his brother, hiding his own feelings of tiredness and fear, encouraged him with hopeful assurances.

For three days they walked on, and for three nights they slept under the stars with Athimoolam's arms held protectively around his brother. As they told their story and asked their way, they received a little food or money from the charitably disposed, or scolding and smacks from the more unfeeling; but still they pressed on.

When they eventually came to the Leprosy Hospital at Vadathorasalur they were awed by the large white buildings and clean paths, and would certainly have passed by, afraid to enter, had they not been fascinated by the boys and girls dressed in blue and white who played happily in the garden with their balls, hula hoops and skipping ropes. Never had they seen children so groomed and neat, and the sight contrasted only too strongly with their own weak bodies, travel-stained clothes and dishevelled appearance.

A few questions from the gate-keeper soon brought out their sorrowful story and within an hour they had been seen by Dr. Pillai and Sister Johanssen; had been washed and reclothed, and taken to the boys' block of the leprosy hospital.

As the child patients of Vadathorasalur sang to me on my visit to their schoolroom I could not pick out the two boys whose story had moved me so much, for *all* the boys and girls looked so happy and well-cared for.

Each year at the Leprosy Home School, which has so great an influence upon the child patients at Vadathorasalur, it is the custom for the youngsters to appoint their own *Balor Saba* or "parliament" and, in 1963, the "Prime Minister" appointed was Athimoolam, the boy whose courage was matched only by his devotion to a younger brother in similar need. He had found the cure for his own fear and gloom in his concern for Marimuthoo and, by his determination, had opened a door of healing and new life for both of them.

THE WORD OF LOVE

"Woman, behold thy son!" — *John 19:26*

Deep pierced the sword into the tender heart
Which long before had trembled at the touch
Of angel visitants; perplexéd much
Had treasured up each secret thought apart:
How vain the balm of dreams to heal the smart;
How aery now the mirage at her clutch:
No crown, save one of thorns; no throne, but such
As fiends would carve in hellish art.
Yet, through the gloom comes soft the piercing beam
To those who stand in silence by the cross,
Commanding each in turn with love's esteem;
Assuaging thus their sore and bitter loss.
So still He mediates His love and care,
Through souls constrained His dying love to share.

2

LOOK UPON MY SON

ONE OF THE FASCINATING aspects of the recorded events in the life of the Lord Jesus is the way in which seemingly epoch-making incidents are followed by what appear to be insignificant or inconsequential trifles. The reason is, of course, that in the purpose of God nothing is inconsequential or trivial, for all events are part of the whole picture in the same way that all strands are part of a tapestry, however great the area of the whole picture, or how slender the strands.

The story of the Transfiguration of our blessed Lord (Luke 9:28-43), is one of the most important events narrated by the Gospel writers, marking, as it does, one of the crucial stages in the revelation of Jesus as the Christ, and the eternal Son of God. On the mountain top, probably Mount Hermon which rises to a height of 9,000 feet above sea-level, the Lord Jesus was transformed so that his garments shone with a dazzling brightness belonging to heaven, rather than the earth. Moses and Elijah appeared with Him, as though holding conference, and a voice came from on high declaring the Sonship and eternal authority of Christ. Moses and Elijah represented the Law and the Prophets as bearing witness to the Messiah whose word and work were to confirm and supersede their own. From the Shekinah cloud, symbolic for centuries of God's presence on earth, the voice said: "This is my beloved Son: hear him" (Mark 9:7), a Son who was to inaugurate the Kingdom with His words, and seal its future victory in His death, resurrection, ascension and final coming in glory.

Immediately after the glorious experience of transfiguration, the Lord Jesus was faced with another "sonship" in a very human situation though Peter, and doubtless the other disciples who witnessed the revelation missed the whole point of the happening. "Master," said Peter to Jesus, "it is good for us to be here; and let us make three tabernacles; one for Thee, and one for Moses, and one for Elias" (Luke 9.33). In other words, "Let us make the revelation a permanent rather than an immediate experience." If we may quote Samuel Greg's lovely paraphrase, his request was:

> Stay, Master, stay upon this heavenly hill
> A little longer, let us linger still
> With all the mighty ones of old beside,
> Near to the aweful Presence we abide;
> Before the throne of light we trembling stand,
> And catch a glimpse into the spirit land.

The poet's insight into the work of the Kingdom of God leads him to suggest the reason why Transfiguration can never be an end in itself, for he goes on:

> "No," saith the Lord, "the hour is past, we go;
> Our home, our life, our duties lie below.
> While here we kneel upon the mount of prayer,
> The plough lies waiting in the furrow there.
> Here, we sought God that we might know His will;
> There, we must do it, serve Him, seek Him still."

The "plough and furrow," in our Lord's case, were represented by a father and a sick child grievously disabled by his illness. A father will accept with stoicism pain and suffering on his own account, but to stand by in helpless agony of mind and heart while a child suffers is beyond the limits of endurance. Their tender years and ignorance of the hard facts of life make children specially vulnerable in times of sickness since they are unable to rationalise their introduction to physical weakness, pain and disability. Some children, indeed, learn to suffer before they have learned to live. Time and location were vastly different between the plains below Mount Hermon in A.D.32 and the foothills of Simla in 1962, but the parallel brought home to me a bridge between the two when I visited the Leprosy Home and Hospital at Subathu. The youngest patient there at the time of my visit was Nartia, a little fellow of nine, whose father, Karnabir, was also a patient. When Karnabir was a boy in one of the Simla villages he paid a visit to a young cousin from whom he caught leprosy. For many years the only treatment he received was what he later called "quack remedies"' which reduced his money rather than the disease. It was not until he was forty-two and a married man with a young family that his disease was taken seriously. His father-in-law, fearing for the health of the family, told the village headman of his disease and he insisted that Karnabir leave the district where he was putting others, including his immediate relatives, at risk.

Begging his way from place to place and becoming progressively weaker, Karnabir came at last to a state of acute despair and longed for death. Climbing the rugged hill paths and crossing boulder-strewn ravines would test any traveller but to one, plagued as he was by foot ulcers, the flinty rocks were an extra hazard he could no longer face and, falling by the wayside, he lay in a pain-wracked stupor, unable to rise. Although some travellers, true to our Lord's parable, "passed by on the other side," one man, a good Samaritan, not only went to his assistance, but also volunteered to turn back on his journey to take the unfortunate sufferer to Subathu.

At the old hill station of Subathu, known to generations of soldiers, leprosy has been treated since 1875 when the Rev. Dr. John Newton, of the American Presbyterian Mission, gathered together a group of leprosy sufferers and accepted responsibility for their care. Dr. Newton had written to Wellesley Bailey, founder of The Leprosy Mission, who had promised to back the effort: "If you are willing to entrust to me the stewardship of such funds, I for my part will thankfully accept the trust." Until his death, five years later, Dr. Newton carried out his promise with faithfulness and zeal and Mr. Bailey echoed the sentiments of the Subathu patients, as well as the Mission supporters, when he wrote: "Who can fill his place? Who will tend them, love them and speak to them as he did? Truly in this blessed work he was largely imbued with his Master's spirit." Fortunately, a succession of faithful men and women, imbued with the same spirit of selfless service, have come forward through the years and the Rev. Dr. Joseph Khan, the latest of these fine Subathu leprosy leaders, was there ready to receive Karnabir when he arrived, weary, sick and very sorrowful.

The treatment and care which Karnabir received at Subathu soon began to affect his leprosy, in spite of the complications brought on by the long years of neglect.

As he grew stronger, the sick man took more and more interest in the hospital which had brought him new hope and, renewed in spirit, he became a staunch worshipper in the hospital church of St. Luke which he came to see as the centre of the hospital's life. No patient sang more lustily, or expressed his joy more feelingly as a member of the church orchestra, than did Karnabir.

Then came the black day when he almost lost his song. A letter arrived from his home with the news that his small son Nartia had fallen victim to the disease which had brought his father to Subathu.

Karnabir was inconsolable. He could face his own sickness but the thought of his young son facing the kind of ostracism which had made his own situation so unbearable was torture to his sensitive spirit.

Dr. Khan suggested that Karnabir should return to his village home and bring back the young lad, promising that early treatment would obviate many of the trials which his own neglected condition had brought to him. Karnabir returned and when I visited Subathu, father and son were together at the Leprosy Hospital, living in a small room adjacent to the men's block. They were in the forefront of the group who welcomed me and I rejoiced to see them at daily worship in the hospital church, or watched them playing together in the compound in the early evening.

On the day of my departure I asked Karnabir if he had a message for the Mission's supporters throughout the world. He smiled broadly as he replied: "May God bless all who are providing for our needs and tell them, 'The Lord be Praised' ". As I left Subathu for the plains below, I looked back and, framed in the gateway of the Hospital, Karnabir and Nartia were standing together, waving farewell.

THE WORD OF SALVATION

"Today shalt thou be with me in paradise"— *Luke 23:43*

Three crosses silhouetted 'gainst the sky,
With felons wiping out by death the score
Of crime; on either side set forth before
The multitude, who came to see them die.
Tongues wag, as mocking laughter hails the cry,
"To seek and save He came! He'll save no more,
Nor save Himself His kingdom to restore-
Perhaps He thinks the cross a panoply!"
Yet He has gained one subject: one who bows
His head, though hands and feet are nailed in place;
He bids his thorn-crowned monarch on him think
And with fast closing lips pays his first vows.
What Kingly love! That even in death's face
Can brave the flood, lest one poor thief should sink.

3

THE MUSIC OF THE HEART

ALL LIFE TENDS to express itself in forms of harmony and music so that even the inanimate becomes symbolic of man's search after concord. This is strikingly brought out in the colloquy between Job and the Lord, as set out in the Old Testament record. The problem facing Job and his friends was that of reconciling belief in God's goodness with the apparently undeserved suffering of people, especially those who sought to love and serve the Almighty. The position of the "suffering good" was made worse by the equally undeserved prosperity of men who were undeniably ruthless, if not unscrupulous. To the three friends of Job the problem was, admittedly, academic and they revelled in their dialectic. For Job, on the other hand, the problem was personal and only too real. It was *his* life that was blasted under the series of cataclysmic events that robbed him of family, livelihood and health. Far from "patient," in the accepted sense of being uncomplaining under affliction, Job clung persistently to his belief in the ultimate goodness of God and it was this patient persistence in a loving purpose which, at length, received its reward.

After three cycles of speeches from his so-called "friends" the patriarch "boils over" in a flood of withering indignation, and appeals to logic and experience to support the view that his suffering is no reflection of personal guilt. He finds peace, not in understanding and explaining the mystery of suffering, but in seeing God at work in his life, with a purpose all-pervading and all-loving (Job 38:1-20). In Dr. A. B. Davidson's words: "The experience of men tells them that they do not reach religious peace through the theoretical solution of problems of providence; the theoretical solution comes later, if it comes at all, through their own reflection upon their history, and the way in which God has led them."

As Job ceases to fight his way through his problems and becomes instead a quiet worshipper, he is given new insights into a view of his own life, set not in isolation, but in a full-orbed recognition of the universe, where even the stars join in an eternal psalm of praise to the Creator and the sea bursts forth to obey the sovereign will. Prophet, poet, and preacher alike have vied with each other in discovering this unity between man, the animate and inanimate creation, and the Creator. They see in the ebb and flow of the tides an echo of the changing moods of life; and in the seasons' progress they find a reflection of the journey of man from his spring to the winter of his discontent, and from his seedtime to the cry of "Harvest Home."

In its kaleidoscopic changes of pattern, life moves, swifter than a shuttle, between the lyric movement of a mountain stream to the vehemence and terror of a raging storm. Do we really find help when we cast back from our own situation of need to the act of creation "When the morning stars sang together, and all the sons of God shouted for joy"? (Job 38:7). Can we find the link between the music of the spheres and the music of the human heart? The witness of Scripture is that we can, and the testimony of countless thousands who have found God in, and through, their suffering, gives assent to the Bible view. "The Lord is my strength and shield," sings the

Psalmist, "my heart trusted in him, and I am helped: therefore my heart greatly rejoiceth, and with my song will I praise him." (Psalm 28:7).

It was such "heart music" which echoed during the midnight hour in the jail at Philippi when neither stripes nor stocks could break the spirit of the missionary pair: "And at midnight Paul and Silas prayed and sang praises unto God; and the prisoners heard them." (Acts 16:25). The same music testifies to the unbroken spirit of our patients who, held captive by disease, and wounded by many stripes laid on them, are able, like Paul and Silas, to sing praises at midnight, awaiting in faith the divine liberation.

Here is a little poem from a child patient, expressing her joy on receiving a new dress from a well-wisher living on the other side of the world:

> 'Tis summer
> This morning
> Blue wind is blowing:
> My dress is red,
> Oh! I'm happy!

The cynic might well ask what she has to be happy about as she faces life, separated from home and loved ones; in the grip of a disease which robs her of so much that makes life meaningful. Like Job, though so much earlier in life, she has found what many men desire and so few find; a grace greater than her need and an inner strength sufficient to turn the mood of sorrow into joy.

The evangelist at the Dichpalli Leprosy Hospital wrote on behalf of other staff and patients testifying: "The day's work rightly begins with singing the praises of our Lord, and with prayers led in turn by members of the staff and some literate Christian patients. Intercessions are made for those who suffer most; and so the day's service ahead is assured of strength from above, and this gives confidence of mind."

Walking round the patients' quarters in the leprosy hospitals of India I was so often struck by the joy expressed in singing, in music, in games and in their forms of communal entertainment. The patients were tireless in their requests, passed on to me through members of staff, that they should sing for me, and the portable tape recorder which I carried everywhere captured, for all time, the unforgettable songs of joy which greeted me. At Champa I heard the child patients singing in their own language groups and we found more than a dozen different language areas of India represented in this one group of boys and girls. The languages differed but the song was one, and for over two hours, the children praised God in happy abandon and only pressure of other engagements on my part brought the session to a close.

At Chandkhuri a small party of girls formed a junior choir and, led by their blind Pastor, Simon Patras, sang to their own accompaniment on a variety of instruments. Their music, together with other singing recorded on the tour, reached a much wider audience when it was later broadcast from London on the B.B.C. network, and the singing created great interest when used to introduce a series of stories from the tour. It surprised many listeners in Great Britain that such happy songs should emanate from leprosy hospitals, and it awakened compassion for the many children who were cared for in the institutions of The Leprosy Mission. In their happy songs the child patients had found the antidote to care and sorrow and music had opened a door into the realm of creative joy.

India's greatest poet, Rabindranath Tagore, says in one of his *Gitanjali* ("Song Offerings") "Ever in my life have I sought thee with my songs . . . It was my songs that taught me all the lessons I have ever learnt; they showed me my secret paths, they brought before my sight many a star on the horizon of my heart . . . They guided me all the day long to the mysteries of the country of pleasure and pain."

In that same music of the heart, we may find an antidote to our own care, and a stimulus for our continued pilgrimage.

THE WORD OF LONELINESS

"My God, my God, why hast Thou forsaken Me?" —
                                        Matt. 27:46

No dial registers the passing hours,
For darkness like a shroud engulfs the hill:
The birds are dumb, the very beasts are still;
The sun, as though in shame, withdraws his dowers
Of light and heat; the city's marts and towers
Are one in darkness with its tombs, until
One word breaks forth, like fire upon the chill,
Cold hearts of those who stand, thralled by death's

                                        powers.

Amazing word! As, when a flower is crushed,
Its essence is distilled upon the air
And death releases fragrance bound in life:
So now, while every earthly sound is hushed;
Th' unutterable woe for man to bear,
He goes, clear-eyed, alone, into the strife.

4

THE POWER OF ENDURANCE

THE POWER OF ENDURANCE is one of the greatest forces in human life, enabling man to cope with, and even overcome, the most intractable elements he is called upon to face. It is not a rebellious endurance which angrily kicks against the goads of life, breeding cynicism and despair, but is rather a moral endurance which makes full use of vicissitudes so that our very difficulties become a stimulus to faith and endeavour.

It was not the groans of the ill-treated prisoners, Paul and Silas, but their midnight songs of praise, which awakened their fellow prisoners in the jail at Philippi. The songs were no acts of bravado, covering-up for latent fear and inner despair, but were the logical outcome of a faith that was buoyant and strong because it had already been tempered in the fires of affliction. Writing eleven years later to the Church at Philippi, which probably included in its membership the jailor who had laid the whip on his back and placed his feet in the stocks, Paul was able to declare: "But I would ye should understand, brethren, that the things which happened unto me have fallen out rather unto the furtherance of the Gospel;" (Philippians 1:12). To one who looked upon himself as "a bondslave of Jesus Christ," even the tribulations and trials which impeded his steps on every side became ladder-rungs by which to mount in victorious living.

Moses was the Old Testament counterpart of Paul and showed similar courageous faith in unpropitious surroundings so that "he endured, as seeing him who is invisible." (Hebrews 11:27). The catalogue of adversities outlined in Hebrews 11 is a worthy parallel to Paul's list of personal misfortunes recorded in 2 Corinthians 4: 8, 9. From birth to death Moses could have echoed every word of the apostle's testimony: "We are troubled on every side, yet not distressed: we are perplexed, but not in despair; persecuted, but not forsaken; cast down, but not destroyed." In his blessing of the tribes whom he had brought, under God, from the bondage of Egypt to the threshold of a new life in Canaan, Moses was only enunciating for their encouragement the aspects of faith and hope which had been his guide and stay through the years: "Bless the Lord, his substance and accept the work of his hands," he counselled Levi. "The beloved of the Lord shall dwell in safety by him," he assured Benjamin. "The Lord is the great provider," he reminded Joseph, Zebulun, Gad and Naphtali. To Asher he gave the loveliest of promises: "As thy days so shall thy strength be," and all the tribes were upon his heart as he closed with a benediction which has brought comfort to every succeeding generation: "The eternal God is thy refuge, and underneath are the everlasting arms:" (Deut. 33:27).

Such matchless faith is not the product of a moment but is the end-product of long endurance, as thousands of Christian leprosy patients and other sufferers can testify. These men and women have endured pain, sorrow and loneliness as the concomitant of physical suffering, yet out of their suffering has come the testimony of God's goodness and mercy.

My stay at the Chandkhuri Leprosy Home and Hospital in Madhya Pradesh, was made memorable by the privilege I had of sharing ministry at different levels, from open-air services for out-patients to staff Bible Classes, with the Rev. Simon Patras, pastor of the centre, who had been blind from birth. He was born into a low-caste, poverty-stricken family near the village of Bisrampur in central India. From the moment of birth the blind baby was treated as a family curse to be rejected as a useless human being who would require food, clothing and special care yet have nothing to offer in return. Unable to read his Bible for himself, Simon developed an acute memory and, since his parents refused to allow him to attend a school for blind children when a place was offered him, he depended more and more on storing up remembered words and phrases. Besides vast quantities of scripture passages he also learned songs, especially those native to his own countryside, and these gave him a wide knowledge of history and religion since these were the primary elements of local lyrics.

By the time he was thirteen the young lad was an ardent disciple and accompanied the Bible women who went from the local Mission station as itinerant preachers into the surrounding villages. His bold declaration that he was going to become a minister when he grew up was tolerated as only a small boy's dream but, when the ambition persisted until it became a major passion of his young life, it was greeted with scorn and derision by his village friends, and by kindly-meant but strong opposition from the missionaries, who thought that his blindness, coupled with his lack of education, would make such a vocation impossible. They had reckoned without Simon's indomitable courage. The young man insisted on enrolling as a candidate village preacher and at the interview which followed, the members of the examining board were so impressed by his intelligent answers, deep knowledge of the scripture and acute spiritual awareness, that they granted him a scholarship for training at a theological seminary.

After having completed his studies, the blind student was ordained as a minister of the Word and Sacraments but the problem still uppermost in the minds of his teachers was to find the young ordinand a post where his gifts could be used in a way that would be unimpeded by his obvious limitations. At the Claire Leprosy Hospital, Chandkhuri, Simon found the perfect setting where his own early struggles, social rejection and physical handicap would be a blessing rather than a hindrance. It was so easy for a man like Simon Patras to minister to men and women suffering in body, mind and spirit because of leprosy. In a very real sense his blindness became an asset, giving him a bond of sympathy, and his courageous victory over his own tragedy added power to his message.

Constantly by his side as he ministers among the patients at Chandkhuri is Reuben, a young lad who acts as secretary, valet, confidant and friend; taking down his sermons, arranging time-tables and seeing to all the things that the blind pastor requires. Besides regular services in the lovely hospital church, Simon teaches geography, history and other subjects in the leprosarium school, gives lessons on hygiene at the out-patient clinics, acts as counsellor and guide to all who seek his advice, and leads Bible classes in a way that makes the Bible a living and relevant power to all who share in the studies.

Following the eastern tradition of preaching, the Pastor dramatises the better-known Bible passages with many telling illustrations from life. Similarly, he uses music effectively to demonstrate the Christian message, and when I was with him at Chandkhuri he used three different musical groups in worship or witness. For the daily church services he had trained an orchestra composed of tabla (drums), tambura and chikari (strings), hand harmonium, and percussion instruments of wood and metal. The anthem was an Indian lyric of his own composition and it was sung by a group of blind and badly crippled patients. Finally, there was a junior orchestra and choir.

Altogether, the ministry of the blind Pastor of Chandkhuri has been of immeasurable value in creating a rich and vigorous spiritual life at the hospital and in the district. Of him it can truly be said: "He endured, as *seeing* him who is invisible" (Heb. 11:27).

THE WORD OF PHYSICAL DESIRE

"Jesus. . .saith, I thirst" — *John 19:28*

Behold Him turn aside His face, when first
The bowl of mingled wine is held aloft
To quench His thirst; benumb in slumbers soft
His aching bones, and end the fire — that worst
Ordeal of flaming head which fain would burst
But cannot for its bonds of flesh. How oft
He promised waters from Life's fount; now scoffed,
He hangs upon the cross and cries: "I thirst"!
Lift high the sponge and press it to His lips
As, in frail flesh, He plumbs the depths of woe,
Gathering strength for that last tide of pain.
They do not, cannot know, who watch Him sip
The cooling draught; He thirsts that they may know
The Fount of Life, and never thirst again.

5

WHEN WE ARE A COMFORT

ONE OF THE FASCINATING THINGS about words is that each one carries with it into vocabulary its own individual background and history. Words having their roots in one country are constantly turning up in the language of another, and words minted for one profession or trade become the adopted "coin" of another.

Every writer learns his trade by using words with the foregoing in mind, choosing and using his words in such a way as to enable them to bring their accumulated usage into his service. The apostle Paul is no exception, and it is clear from his letters that he chooses his words with knowledge and care from history and experience, from law and the learned professions, from the university and from the market place.

In his letter to the Colossians we have one of the words which he probably gained from his conversations with his "beloved physician", Luke. Writing from Rome to his friends in Colossae, he lists the people whose kindly presence he misses during his involuntary exile, remarking: "These only are my fellow workers unto the kingdom of God, which have been a comfort unto me" (Colossians 4:11). "These... have been a comfort unto me," he writes, knowing that the medical word he uses for "comfort" will be recognised in the sense a doctor or dispenser would use it. It is the word from which we get "paregoric" — "a healing cordial". How often his painful eyes had been eased by herbal infusions that brought unbelievable relief in their laving! How often under the care of Luke, cordials and balms had brought relief to nerves inflamed by illness and anxiety! How often the fevered body, tortured by pain, had lapsed into a dreamless oblivion of peace, under thoughtful medication.

Now he thinks of the friends whose loving concern, and generosity with time and money, are bringing compensation for his loss of liberty, and he likens the aid which his friends are giving to a paregoric draught of healing and comfort. How much we owe to these "paregoric souls", these ministering angels. Like "a certain Samaritan" who carried "oil and wine" with him on his journey, they take with them day by day the means of comfort in case they come upon a traveller in need. Forgetful of their own burdens they cheerfully lend their shoulders to those who fall under heavier loads; ignoring their own needs, they find joy in sharing with others anything that they possess.

In the hands of such "comforters" the cordial of love becomes an antidote for the poison of bitterness and a source of strength. Kind thoughts and gentle action are agencies of healing; by them the fever of discontent is calmed, and the stings of life lose their power to hurt. "Through such souls alone," teaches Robert Browning, "God, stooping down, shows sufficient of His light for us in the dark to rise by." In the important "Rolls of Honour", collated in this world, the "comforter" seldom has a place, but in God's more exact record, as in St. Paul's letter, those who "have been a comfort" are remembered against oblivion.

Often when I have known the name of a doctor, a surgeon or a missionary nurse, I have wished also to have the name of some nurse-aide, paramedical worker, compounder, technician, Bible woman or clerk and was always glad when such found a place in the Annual Reports from leprosy centres. I well remember the day when a group of eight old and crippled patients from Kalimpong arrived in Purulia after a long and trying journey lasting more than four days. They had been evacuated because of the threat of a Chinese invasion from the North and, after travelling hundreds of miles by boat, train and bullock-cart, they eventually arrived at the Purulia Leprosy Hospital tired, dirty, and in need of medical care.

I saw two young nurse-aides, patients themselves, stripping dirty bandages from the legs of two old Nepali women who were in the party. Talk was impossible because neither of the girls knew a word of Nepali, the only language known to Budhimaya and Tshering Khipa, the two women evacuees, and the job was loathsome because of the long days and nights of neglect. Yet the girls smiled happily and treated the elderly patients with a respect and care worthy of a daughter-mother relation.

I remembered a similar instance when a visitor from overseas had stood in an ulcer clinic watching two young nurses at work. In English the visitor had whispered to a member of staff: "I would not be able to do that for a thousand pieces of gold." One of the young nurses looked up, her sparkling eyes and winsome smile informing him that she had heard and understood, for only her illness had caused her to exchange college for hospital. Then she answered, softly, "Neither would I do it for gold! Only love makes it possible."

The young nurses, like so many I met on my visits to leprosy centres, had found the secret of "being a comfort", and this is worth much more than silver and gold.

An Indian minister once told me of the time when he was invited to become chaplain of a leprosy Home whereupon he visited the institution, even though he had already decided in his own mind to turn the invitation down. His fear was so great that at Sunday worship he turned over the pages of the pulpit Bible thinking, "How many leprous hands have touched this book?" During his stay at the leprosy Home he watched the "patient-Guides" on parade and at play, noticing particularly a young missionary nurse who had joined the patients at netball. As she threw — and received — the ball he was astounded that a girl should travel thousands of miles to serve *his* people and be unafraid of disease, while he, a national, had been filled with fear. His own fear was dispelled, cancelled out by love, and for many years he served the leprosy patients in the hospital with zeal and compassion.

It was India's greatest Poet, Rabindranath Tagore, who said, in one of his *Gitanjali ("Song offerings")*;

"Here is thy footstool and there rest thy feet where live the poorest, and lowliest, and lost.
When I try to bow to thee, my obeisance cannot reach down to the depth where thy feet rest among the poorest, and lowliest and lost.
Pride can never approach to where thou walkest in the clothes of the humble among the poorest,
and lowliest and lost.
My heart can never find its way to where thou keepest company with the companionless among the poorest, the lowliest, and the lost."

It is this spirit of comfort which most meets the needs of our patients, and those who offer it find a reward far too adequate for the service they render. Without the ministry of comfort what would all our medical care and surgical skill amount to? Only as the medicine and surgery, the physiotherapy and the social work are passed through the sieve of love can they be purified and made fit to be channels of Him who sets us both the task and the example. He it is who is the ultimate source of comfort and in Him we shall find our ministry bearing fruit, to our encouragement and to His glory.

THE WORD OF FULFILMENT

"Jesus. . . said, It is finished:" — John 19:30

Behold Him there, the heir of David's line:
Upon His rough-hewn throne transfixed before
The soulless multitude. No servitor
To do Him reverence, human or divine.
In Him, the priest and victim both combine
Man to redeem, the Father to adore.
The prophet's vision, all the hidden love
Of ages past, fulfilled in one design.
As Son of Man, the tale is finished now.
'Twixt the poor stable and the lonely cross
As David's son, with thorn-encircled brow,
Ended the scorn and the so bitter loss.
As Son of God fulfilled the eternal vow,
Refined the heavenly gold from earthly dross.

6

BLAMING THE SOWER FOR THE SOIL

THE CYNIC and the pessimist *must* get a good deal of gratuitous pleasure out of reading the parable of the sower (Matthew 13:3-9). How typical of life's frustrations, they say, as they contemplate the scene. The sower, full of hope and encouraged by his inner vision of overflowing barns, went out with his seedbasket to broadcast the seed over the land, and what happened? "Some fell by the wayside," on impervious soil trodden by the feet of workmen until it is hard as rock. Almost before the seed has reached such ground, the birds have swooped upon it and devoured it. "Some fell upon stony places, where they had not much earth." Here, with slightly better conditions the seeds do germinate, but not to much purpose. Root and shoot are pathetically poor and prove no match for the burning sun which shines down upon the hard shelf of rock with its thin covering of earth. All too soon the tiny roots give up the struggle and the infant plants wither away. "Some fell among the thorns, and the thorns sprung up and choked them." Even when established in the ground the young plants must inevitably join existing growth in the battle for existence. Surrounded by noxious, strangling weeds, what chance has the seed for progressive growth? The weeds may not have too much future but the present seems to belong to them, and the good seed must fight them for a place in the sun.

If that were the whole story we would seem to be

working towards ultimate failure and despair, but there is more, and better, news to follow in the parable of Jesus, for He continues: "Other (seed) fell into good ground, and brought forth fruit." When you have catalogued all the disabilities there is still an asset side to the ledger of life. If there are situations which militate against growth and fruitfulness, there is also good ground which is capable of producing valuable crops, "some an hundredfold, some sixtyfold, some thirtyfold."

In the parable of the sower, you will remember, the seed and the sower are the same in every case. It is the soil and the circumstances which vary. I find it significant that in the modern field of cybernetics and computer statistics it is necessary to distinguish between "basics" and "variables." The basics are constant and unalterable, while the variables must be adjusted day by day as new facts come to light. The vocabulary may, indeed, change but the lessons of the parable of the sower are surprisingly up-to-date. The seed and the sower are the "basics" while the wayside, the birds and the thorns etc., are the "variables." It is the soil-situation which is the key, varying as it does from rocky outcrop, through weed-producing clay and silt, to rich humus-bearing loam.

On my India tour I was fascinated by the constant stories I was told of poor non-agricultural land — bought cheaply because it had been neglected — which by patient husbandry (using patient in both of its senses) had been turned into productive units of great value.

The classic example was at Faizabad. The Rev. Wilfrid H. Russell, the first Superintendent of the Faizabad project, had described the site chosen as "of poor quality because it was what was known locally as *nuna* or *usar* land, which means land with a lot of salt in it. Such land can be reclaimed by ploughing-in leguminous crops, and by thorough irrigation which will in time wash the salt away. The local villagers could not afford to invest capital or labour in land of such poor quality and that is why it was abandoned."

Mr. Russell was referring to the land, almost fifty acres, as it existed when it was taken over by the Mission, and about twenty-five years were to pass before I visited Faizabad when the wilderness had indeed blossomed as the rose. With justifiable pride Dr. Patrick showed me the operation of the irrigation plant which carried water to every part of the Faizabad site, and I saw for myself the sugar cane plantation which has gained such high praise in an area where such crops are a staple commodity. The first Medical Superintendent of Faizabad, Dr. P. J. Chandy, was known locally as "Farmer Chandy" because of the success that followed his land reclamation scheme.

The irrigated earth, with its production of sweet cane, fruits, vegetables and flowers, is not the only soil, or even the primary "soil" of Faizabad, just as the earth by the shores of the Sea of Galilee was not the only "soil" in the mind of the Lord Jesus as he watched the sower and used his efforts as a parable in His teaching.

I like the imagery used by an anonymous modern poet as he pondered the parable of the sower:

> Somewhere upon a bare hillside
> Above the lake that gleam'd below
> A peasant sowed at morning-tide
> His field, and Jesus watched him sow.
>
> Far are the hills of Galilee,
> That harvest long is reaped: but still
> Jesus is watching us, as we
> Sow in *His* field for good or ill.

For all our thoughts and words are seeds,
And still we scatter as we go,
And happy lives or evil deeds
Spring from the kind of seed we sow.

Our secret thoughts will germinate,
And spoken words set something growing;
God give us grace that love, not hate,
May be the harvest of our sowing.

The true harvest of Faizabad is not to be found in its measures of grain, or sugar cane, though these are evidences of God's guiding hand. The true harvest lies in the lives of patients who have been helped to new life: the boys and girls who have occupied, successively, the Wellesley Bailey Children's Sanatorium; the older patients who have passed through the hospital wards and returned to their own villages with restored bodies and cheerful hearts; the crowds of out-patients who have reaped the benefit of years of research into the cause and cure of leprosy.

This is the harvest which we can now see as the fruit of the years, and it is that harvest which will, in the end, qualify for the Master's commendation: "Well done, thou good and faithful servant: thou hast been faithful over a few things... enter thou into the joy of thy Lord." (Matthew 25:21).

THE WORD OF RECONCILIATION

"Jesus... said, Father, into Thy hands
I commend my spirit:" — Luke 23:46

Into the hands from whence thou first didst come,
Give thou thyself against corruption's power;
Victor thou art in evil's mighty hour,
Though hell's armed legions seek to overcome
Thou wilt not vainly to their toils succumb.
Death waits upon thee, eager to devour
While earth stands darkened in a sunless hour
And heaven prepares a rich encomium.
What words are there upon the silent air?
No victory for death the words portend,
But livelier tones faith's victory declare:
"Into Thy hands, O Father, I commend,
Knowing I cannot lose thy loving care,
My spirit when this earthly life shall end."

7

HUMAN TOIL AND DIVINE GLORY

IT WAS A GREAT DAY for Israel when the work of building the tabernacle was completed in the wilderness. To have accomplished such a task while travelling through the desert which lay between Egypt and Canaan was a tremendous achievement in itself, for materials were limited, and many that must have seemed necessary for the task were non-existent.

Only scrubland trees like the Shittim or Acacia were available to be cut down for the altar and other sections of the tabernacle, and even then the wood required strengthening by metal overlay, copper for the court and gold for the altar and holy table. The metal itself was obtained by the collection of offerings varying from the silver redemption money to the donation of vanity mirrors. The women supplied both material and service for the curtains, including "the curtains of the tent" which were of goat's hair, ram's skin and linen, and the ornately embroidered veil which was to hang between the holy of holies and the holy place. Each piece of furniture was made with loving care and meticulous accuracy, according to the "blueprint" which Moses brought from Mount Sinai. There was a magnificent altar-chest containing emblems of faith and hope, vessels for worship and sacrifice, together with a golden candelabra for the illumination of the inner sanctuary.

Now the work was complete and for the first time the work of many hands over many months was "on show" to the tribes, and was ready for its dedication. "So Moses finished the work," is the modest reference of the sacred historian and if the matter had ended there it would still have been a wonderful achievement. However, this was not the end, but a new beginning in Israel's religious life, for the historian proceeds: "So Moses finished the work. Then a cloud covered the tent of the congregation, and the glory of the Lord filled the tabernacle". (Exodus 40: 33,34).

There lies the secret of Moses' insistence that the pattern of the mount be followed with scrupulous care. The presence of the Shekinah glory, within and above the tabernacle their hands had made, symbolized the complete blending of human toil and divine glory in one eternal relevance. All that man had done, from the earliest planning and provision of materials to the erection and dedication of the completed sanctuary, gave witness to God's desire for co-operation among men, for Him and with Him. God, in His sovereignty, could have delivered a sanctuary to earth like some new Jerusalem, descending through the open skies. Instead, He encouraged their devotion and service.

Silver and gold, ram's skin dyed red, acacia wood and embroidered linen, all have their place in the making of Israel's "tent of congregation." Likewise every group, and every tribe, had a part to play. Only the Levites could minister in the sanctuary, but every family was called upon for the silver redemption money which was later to become foundation sockets for the sanctuary; half a shekel for each person aged twenty or older. Specialist craftsmen, working in gold and silver were given responsibility for the fashioning of ornate jewellery, chains, and the crowns with which the tabernacle furniture was surmounted. The seamstresses also had a part to play in making the curtains and hanging screens.

It is part of the Divine dignity and condescension that when He would reveal His glory in some new way He inspires His children to pray, to give and to serve, that His glory shall have a channel through which it can be revealed to the world.

Note that it was when "Moses finished the work" the Shekinah glory was revealed and a radiance richer than that of sun or moon enveloped the tabernacle area, covering the work of man with Heaven's brightness. How involved had been the directions given! What folly it had seemed to build under wilderness conditions! How much more convenient it would have been to settle in Canaan before building a sanctuary! As always, God's ways reveal a purpose greater than we can understand: "For my thoughts are not your thoughts, neither are your ways my ways, saith the Lord. For as the heavens are higher than the earth, so are my ways higher than your ways, and my thoughts than your thoughts" (Isaiah 55: 8,9).

It is our task, surely, to interpret His revealed will to the best of our ability and then to follow that will in loving service. In other words we are here to build His sanctuary, and when we have done *all* that we can do, His glory will overshadow our human efforts, transforming earthly toil into a heavenly Kingdom.

If only we could see, accept and fulfil our part in Christian work, how challenging our service would become and with what radiance it would be enobled in its conclusion!

The part we play may not seem important, but so long as it is the part He has chosen for us we can continue our work with assurance. The work of Bezaleel, the goldsmith and Aholiab, the engraver, may have *seemed* more important than that of the nameless women who were to sew 5-cubit high curtains for the 100 × 50-cubit sides of the tabernacle court, but on the day of dedication the radiance of God "covered the tent of the congregation, and the glory of the Lord filled the tabernacle" (Exodus 40:34).

We need the hands of the brilliant surgeon for the reconstructive operations carried out in the hospital, but we also need the hands of a junior clerk to type out the letter of thanks which will gladden the heart of a faithful supporter in an isolated hamlet at home. We need the healing hands of the nurse as she lessens the fever in a case of fierce reaction, but we also need the hands of the deputation worker manipulating the projector which screens the film illustrating her work. We need the calm resolute hands of the physiotherapist seeking to bring new life into muscles long inactive, but we also need the excited hands of a little child placing coins in the collecting box at a village school or church.

The hands which God brings together in our healing programme are as varied as the countries and situations which they represent. Let us have in our thoughts the quick brown hands of an Indian paramedical worker, out on a village survey, moving over the body, seeking signs of a disease he may once have feared. Let us remember the clawing hands of the Bible Woman who came much too late for tendon transplants, muscle grafts and the sophisticated procedures by which so many patients are being helped to-day, yet thanks God that her damaged hands hold a Bible from which she draws the inspiration and knowledge which will bring comfort to others.

Let us remember, above all, the many hands outstretched in a piteous plea for help; hands so young, as men count life by years, but already old in neglect and ultimate uselessness. If we and others are alert, the radiance of God will come even upon such hands, bringing healing and new life. If we but build, regardless of cost or consequence, there will come a day when His "cloud" will cover our "tent" and we shall see His glory in the fulfilment of His purpose.

HIS BROKEN BODY — OUR ONENESS

"That they may be one" — John 17:11

The incense clouds from myriad altars raised
Rise heav'nward till they mingle at Thy Throne;
Ten thousand tongues all blend, though oft unknown
As Thou, from West to mystic East art praised!
By broken bread Thine own were once amazed
But now the simple sign Thy faithful own
Where many meet, or one saint stands alone,
Content to know that on Thy face he's gazed.
What though the ways of human life divide
By sea's engulfing, and loud Babel's ire;
Our common need brings us to Thee our guide,
And we are fused in love's eternal fire.

8

THE FIELD IS THE WORLD

THE TOUCHSTONE of the Gospel is the declaration that "God so loved the world" (John 3:16), but it is doubtful if, after two thousand years of Christian teaching, we are much nearer a truly global faith. This is not strange since the disciples, who had the advantage of intimate day-by-day fellowship, stumbled at this very "stone" of offence. The Lord Jesus saw a kind of global significance in the individual, as a study of the Gospel narratives proves again and again.

An obvious example is the story of our Lord's one contact with a Samaritan woman which coloured His teaching for days after the event (John 4:31-42). The disciples had left their Master seated by a well-head at the approach to the village of Sychar. When they left Him, He was in a state of extreme fatigue yet, on their return, they found Him animated, vital and enthusiastic. Their first reaction was that he had partaken of food and that this, together with the rest, had changed his weariness to euphoria. It was, in fact, exhilaration produced by a vision of His Kingdom! One Samaritan woman, brought face to face with her own spiritual needs, had led Him to consider the spiritual hunger of the whole world. The woman came from a needy village, in a needy country, in a needy world; the world He had come to save!

In Judaea and Samaria, among Jews and Gentiles alike, there were open wounds that cried out for healing; there were aching hearts burdened by guilt that grace could restore; there were hands outstretched in piteous pleas for help and salvation. "Lift up your eyes", He calls to His disciples, "and look on the fields: for they are white already to harvest!" (John 4:35).

A few days later, surrounded by the sick, the sinful and the needy in His native Galilee, He is still thinking of the individual in global terms, and he yearns that His disciples shall catch the vision before it is too late. "The harvest truly is plenteous, but the labourers are few," He tells them, "Pray ye therefore the Lord of the harvest, that he will send forth labourers into his harvest." (Matthew 9:37,38).

From the individuals who were finding healing and peace, His thoughts turned constantly to the many who were still beyond the reach of His voice and the touch of His hands. The plight of the crowds filled Him with a sorrow almost too heavy to bear, and He groaned in the spirit at the toll of disease and sin in human life so that "he was moved with compassion on them, because they fainted, and were scattered abroad, as sheep having no shepherd." (Matthew 9:36).

As He interprets the parable of the tares in the field He reiterates the thought so often in His mind: "the field is the world," (Matthew 13:38), and when His followers see the first-fruits of their own ministry He is in an ecstasy of exaltation and says, "I beheld Satan as lightning fall from heaven" (Luke 10:18) as though their earthly service held a cosmic significance.

It is easy for us to become elated over the blessing which attends the work of The Leprosy Mission and similar agencies but it is salutary to remember how great is the backcloth of need against which our efforts are set. For those already under our care the hope of full health becomes more and more promising, but such words as healing, cure, rehabilitation, and spiritual good, still have little or no meaning for the vast majority of leprosy sufferers in the world. At a conference of leprosy workers gathered at Purulia in 1963, Dr. Ernest Muir. doyen of leprologists, looked back to his own efforts in West Bengal over many years and likened leprosy to mushrooms growing in a field. "One day," he said, "you visit the field and cut out the mushrooms saying, 'now the field is clear,' but, alas, the following day when you visit the field, not only are there mushrooms wherever you cut them out yesterday, but there are new patches of growth that did not exist the day before." In West Bengal and Bihar, where Dr. Muir and his successors laboured for so many years, leprosy is still a major problem. In the whole of India there are still some three and a half million leprosy sufferers, of whom about 400 thousand are able to spread the infection because of their condition.

The Survey, Education and Treatment Centres (SET), which are a major part of the Indian Government's anti-leprosy plan, are already bringing good results and Christian Missions are wholeheartedly behind, and within, the national scheme. To be with a village SET group as the members take part in control visitation is to see the very heart of leprosy work but, as each worker covers a population from 15 to 20,000, the task is formidable in a country of about 600 million people. We need to pray that sufficient workers, sufficient wisdom, and sufficient compassion and enthusiasm, will be available to see the national plan carried to its conclusion.

The stories I have told in this book have been drawn almost entirely from India but we cannot forget that, as with the preaching of the Gospel, so with leprosy care and control, "the field is the world." Fifteen million or more leprosy sufferers are involved to some degree when we speak of the ramifications of the disease. In a sense in which they could never have appealed to our forefathers, the sombre facts appeal to us, saying: "If thou wilt, thou canst make me clean," (Mark 1:40). As never before, we have the means at our disposal. May we have the will to see them used, until the day dawns when leprosy will no more be feared in the countries of the world where it is a menace today. "The field is the world," and it is the world which God so loved that He sent the Saviour down to share in its life and to die for its salvation.

BY GALILEE

There is a lad here, which hath five barley loaves,
and two small fishes:" — John 6:9.

Long years ago, while fast the sun was sinking,
A boy brought loaves, and laid them at His feet:
"Naught else have I but these, my simple offering,
In answer to Thy call, 'Give them to eat'."

The Master paused, and raised His hands in blessing
Sending the bread, the hungry crowd to feed:
Five simple loaves, His own rich grace possessing,
Were now enough to meet the greatest need.

Lord, take my life, each gift, each talent using
As all are magnified by Thy great love,
And, as I fill the place of Thine own choosing,
Feed Thou the crowds with manna from above.

9

THE EVERLASTING ARMS

IT WAS A TENDER CONSIDERATION on the part of Moses when, having bestowed his farewell blessing on the individual tribes of Israel, he gave a final benediction to the whole people under the group name of Jeshurun. One by one, the great tribal families had been singled out for special mention by the patriarch as he recalled moments in their history with the precision of a scholar and the admiration of a father. Now, in poetic, if cryptic language, he offers his closing benediction, gathering them all into the fold of God's affection: "There is none like unto the God of Jeshurun, who rideth upon the heaven in thy help, and in his excellency on the sky. The eternal God is thy refuge, and underneath are the everlasting arms." (Deuteronomy 33:26,27).

The word "Jeshurun" is a kind of pet-name for Israel and it occurs only four times in the Old Testament. Its literal meaning is "the God of the beloved ones," so the sense of the phrase used by Moses in his gracious benediction is a view of a God whose love is revealed in strong arms outstretched in comfort and support. Readers of Rudyard Kipling will perhaps recall the tense and poignant scene in his story *The Light that Failed* where an artist, suddenly conscious that he is losing his sight, cries out in despair: "Hold me! This darkness seems something I am about to fall through." It is at such times of personal despair that we need to be assured of "the everlasting arms" for it is God's answer to the need of man. It is His strength coming to the aid of our weakness; it is His light cleaving the darkness; it is His assurance banishing disaster's bitter cry. How often our leprosy patients must have been brought to near despair! Their little, personal world must seem to disintegrate as the stark realisation of leprosy breaks upon the numb spirits of the afflicted. The more sensitive the spirit, the more painful must be the initial shock of knowing that the disease has been contracted.

I remember meeting such a person at Vadathorasalur, in South India. Sundari had been a patient for only a few months when I visited the hospital, and, after a quiet conversation in the schoolroom where she had just finished a teaching session with some of the younger patients, she wrote out for me her own story. Her manuscript began: "Life histories are usually written by men and women of great intelligence and accomplishment, but I am a girl of simple tastes, and am only eighteen years of age. Nevertheless, I feel that the story I am telling you may have a value, if only to bear testimony to the grace of the Lord Jesus Christ, which has been a great source of strength in years of suffering and difficulty."

Sundari's family had been involved in the life of the Indian Army from the days of Queen Victoria, and one relative had, in fact, received the Victoria Cross for his outstanding valour on the battle field. Her father had turned aside from military pursuits and, after having left university, had become an engineer with special responsibility for housing and social development. It was this involvement with social needs which brought him into contact with Mahatma Gandhi, so much so that he joined the Mahatma in the famous Satyagraha fire incident. As a result, Ghandhi and his disciple were both thrown into

Yervada Jail, Bombay, in 1930. Further periods in jail followed, including a seven years imprisonment for radicalism, but this only strengthened him in his fight for social justice.

Growing up in such an atmosphere led Sundari to think always of the needs of others, and she trained at school and college with the aim of serving her people in some department of social development. It was while she was working, in Madras, for her B.Sc. in Domestic Science that she was called into the office of the college Principal. Were the term marks unsatisfactory? Had she failed in some matter of conduct? Was there, perhaps, bad news from home? A thousand questions raised their heads as she entered the office!

"You have been to the sickroom about your forehead?" asked the Principal, but there was a gravity about the way the question was asked.

"Yes," answered Sundari, "but I expect it is nothing." Trying to hide her concern over the small, but growing, white patch, she went on:

"I only asked for some cosmetic powder to hide it until it went away of its own accord."

"We fear the patch is an early sign of leprosy" was the reply, "so we must make absolutely sure before you continue your studies at the college."

The fears of countless generations centred in the cry which came from the student but the Principal was inexpressibly kind, as was her father when he accompanied Sundari to the Leprosy Hospital at Vadathorasalur, where she was advised to become an in-patient. The medicines and the wax-bath treatment which were available brought signs of recovery, and stayed the hand-involvement which Sundari had put down to over indulgence in sport, but which was, in reality, the onset of claw hand, a tragic result of the leprosy bacillus damaging the peripheral nerves, bringing wasting and atrophy to the muscles. Sundari began to realise that she was fortunate in having such a quick diagnosis of early leprosy and, as her spirit recovered, she gladly accepted some responsibility for teaching younger patients.

"Because I have had the privilege of a good education I am able to help in the school at Vadathorasalur," she told me, "and also I am able to help in the gardens to keep the Home beautiful. We have, as you know, a beautiful church on the compound and I pray every day that I might be given grace and patience to wait for the time to come when I can return to my college studies and my home."

I could see that the few months at Vadathorasalur had made a great difference to Sundari as the healing balm of Christian compassion was wedded to the medical skill and nursing care. She had, indeed, found "the everlasting arms" at a time when faith, hope and love were all under attack. In such places as Vadathorasalur there is enrichment for staff as well as patients. The courage and fortitude of the patients in their adversity become a challenge and a benediction to the staff, confirming them in their discipleship. As they watch people like Sundari, slowly making a conquest over their vicissitudes, they glory in the triumph, mirrored in Mary Webb's moving poem,

A Factory of Peace

I watched her in the loud and showery lanes
Of life; and every face that passed her by
Grew calmly restful, smiling quietly,
As though she gave, for all her griefs and pains,
Largesse of comfort, soft as summer rains,
And balsam tinctured with tranquility,
Yet in her own eyes dwelt an agony.
"Oh, halcyon soul," I cried, "What sorrow reigns
In that calm heart which knows such ways to heal?"
She said — "Where balms are made for human uses,
Great furnace fires, and wheel on grinding wheel
Must crush and purify the crude herb juices,
And in some hearts the conflicts cease:
They are the sick world's factories of peace."

THE HOLY GRAIL

*"The man in whose hand the cup is found, he shall
                    be my servant;" — Gen 44: 17.*
*"And he took the cup . . . and gave it to them, saying
                    Drink ye all of it;" — Matt 26: 27.*

Lord, give me grace the cup to take,
This Holy Grail of love.
Help me the sacrifice to make,
Demanded from above.

The cup shall be the outward sign
Of bonds no man can see;
Of servitude to love Divine,
Thy slave's best liberty.

'Twas for my sake within the grove
Thine own dread cup was passed;
In vain satanic forces strove,
Love's "I will," held Thee fast.

So is it now with me, dear Lord,
I take the cup and drink.
Low at Thy feet with broken sword
But radiant face, I sink.

Then as I rise and leave the shrine
Give me the Grail to keep;
Let it remind me I am Thine,
My "Sacramentum" deep.

10

READY SANDALS

THE SOUTH INDIAN BOY looked up from his Tamil Bible. He had been fascinated by the stories of the Apostle's missionary journeys, following them, not only in the pages of the New Testament but also on a map which he found on the wall of the hospital chapel. Coming to the words recorded in Acts 21, verse 13 he read them aloud, as though they were a key, opening up the whole passage: "for I am ready not to be bound only, but also to die at Jerusalem for the name of the Lord Jesus." The young lad paused in his reading and his eyes sparkled as though they would take in not only the walled courtyard where he sat but also the distant hills that filled the horizon and, beyond them, the vast world he knew only by books and in his imagination. Time, no less than space, ceased to have significance for him. He was in India only in body, for his heart was fired with the long journeys through Asia Minor about which he was reading. He was a child of the twentieth century with a limited experience, even of his own country, but his mind was forced back to the first century of the Christian era. In church the Pastor had explained the Apostle's thinking in the Acts of the Apostles and his letters to the Churches, illustrating his message with a chain of association which included the Apostle's analogy linking the Christian life with the battle accoutrements of a Roman centurion: "Wherefore take unto you the whole armour of God . . . having your loins girt about with truth, and having on the breastplate of righteousness; and your feet shod with the preparation of the Gospel of peace." (Ephesians 6: 13-15). "Paul had ready sandals," the Pastor had said, as the pictures from Acts and Ephesians merged into one. "The Lord give us all ready sandals!" whispered one of the group who had listened to the Pastor's comment, "Christ has so many unready followers. We don't want to add to their number!"

Those *ready sandals* became a kind of preoccupation with me on my India journey. From the Punjab to Madras and West Bengal to Bombay, I saw in all the leprosy centres the sandal-makers at work. Sometimes the work was primitive; just a slice of unwanted car-tyre and whipcord thonging; at other times elaborate, close-fitting sandals that were as decorative as they were remedial, coloured leather for the fashion conscious, matched with the correct micro-cellular rubber, cork and latex insole, together with such other aids as orthopaedic skill and scientific "know-how" can bring to bear upon the problem of insensitive and ulcerated feet.

As early as 1953 when The Leprosy Mission and American Leprosy Missions Inc. held an International Leprosy Conference at Lucknow, Uttar Pradesh, India, Dr. Paul Brand was reporting on the attempts which he and his colleagues were making at Vellore "to investigate the whole problem of upper and lower limb paralysis, anaesthesia, absorption, contracture and deformity," and seeking "to find methods of prevention of deformity where it can be prevented, of cure of the deformity where it can be cured, and of the alleviation of the disability of the patient from the deformity where cure is impossible."

Dr. Joseph S. Khan was the first of our mission doctors I was to see in action at his hospital at Subathu in North India. Indeed, he was one of the pioneers of "rest therapy" for trophic ulcers, placing the foot and leg in a protective casing of plaster of Paris instead of loose bandages, and he, along with our other doctors, has shared in the great advances in the care of feet deformed, damaged, or at risk through leprosy.

In more recent days we have seen the surgeon, the physiotherapist, and prosthetist, working as a team to carry out the ideals outlined by Paul Brand at the Lucknow Conference. All over the world the "doctrine of the first ulcer" is being taught as a primary safeguard in early leprosy, while physiotherapy and re-constructive surgery have extended the possibilities of rehabilitation for thousands of patients who would otherwise have been crippled for life.

The greatest cause of foot damage is the neglect of the initial ulcer which may be very small and easily cured. The fact that it is there at all is a warning to the patient that his foot is at risk, even though leprosy may have taken away his feeling and made him oblivious of the ulceration.

If, however, the first ulcer is neglected others will follow and eventually may lead to the complete destruction of a foot. When you see a man whose legs have been amputated it is sad to have to trace the trouble back to one early ulcer. I was not surprised to see the earnestness with which the physiotherapists proclaimed this truth by word of mouth, cartoon posters and lessons from life, in order "by all means to save some." Patients have to be taught that even a sandal will not prevent damage to an anaesthetic foot if a stone is embedded in the insole, or a nail or thorn has passed through the outer sole. They are advised to inspect their sandals and their feet, morning and evening, pressing their thumbs over the danger zones as they have seen the leprosy workers do.

Only thus can the "ready sandals" fulfil their purpose.

At all the leprosy centres which I visited I was taken very early on the visit, to the shoe-makers' shops; sometimes a small hut where the workers, often patients, sat cross-legged on the ground making sandals and shoes. On other occasions, especially at the larger centres, the shoe-workshop was filled with the hum and clatter of machines, from the do-it-yourself version to the sophisticated machine, made available on the advice of internationally known manufacturers. It is not for nothing that Paul Brand advised his student shoe-makers that "it is worthwhile being on good terms with a local shoe factory." A last, discarded by a manufacturer can be adapted; off-cuts of no value to a commercial firm can be adjusted; and an outmoded machine replaced in a modern shoe-factory can be made to complete new tasks. Many such samples were shown to me with understandable pride. "We always use coloured leather for our sandals so that, instead of our sandals marking their wearers as obvious leprosy patients, even strangers say, 'Where can I buy a pair like yours?'" This explanatory remark was made to me when I admired the skins of blue, red and green which were being cut into strips at one of our leprosy hospitals in South India.

There was compassion as well as psychological insight in the preference for colour. Unfortunately, a good sandal has been known to defeat its object by the very attraction of the finished product and I was told of one patient who left the leprosy hospital with his feet firmly planted in his first protective sandals. On his next visit to the out-patient clinic some weeks later, the foot showed signs of inflammation and a new ulcer was causing the patient to limp. Questioning by a puzzled worker soon elicited the information that the patient reserved his lovely sandals for going to church and visiting the clinic! It had been unthinkable to use such sandals in the fields or at the bazaar! After a rebuke from the doctor, and a further visit to the shoemaker, the patient, now a sadder but wiser man, promised to take not one single step without the protection of his sandals. When you pray for our missionary doctors, nurses, physiotherapists and other professionally trained workers, will you please remember the non-professional worker-patients whom they train? The skill and expertise which they often acquire is wedded to a devotion which comes from their desire to serve their brethren.

Helped to new life and health themselves, they take a special pride in being able to assist others. Sometimes, indeed, they themselves are badly crippled and the relief and capability which they ensure for their fellow-patients is beyond their own reach; but this situation is taken as a spur, encouraging them to greater efforts on the part of others, lest they too become crippled.

At Vellore Christian Medical College, John Girling, who has made a study of foot problems since being introduced to the work by Paul Brand, demonstrated for me the modern techniques of diagnosis. Using a vulcanised rubber foot-print pad covered with printer's ink he showed how a footprint trail could be made by making a patient walk across the mat and then across the floor. The footprint trail reveals the distribution of pressure by leaving light and dark areas in the "printed step," like a fingerprint writ large! The areas are easily analysed and can help the doctor, physiotherapist and shoe-maker in their work of healing and rehabilitation. Following upon this simple printing mat has come the electronic pressure register. Tiny electrodes are fixed to the various pressure points on the patient's foot and, as he walks across the room, highly sensitive needles flash across the dials of the monitoring machine indicating the thrust and shear of the component parts of the foot as they move, in harmony or hostility according to the disability or well-being of the foot.

Thanks to this sophisticated type of investigation, more and more leprosy patients are being helped towards the prevention of deformity and disability. Apart from the fact that leprosy sufferers often feel no pain, there is no place where the words of Canon Twells find greater fulfilment than in the foot clinic of a modern leprosy hospital: "O in what divers pains they met! O with what joy they went away!"

To see the limping patients coming along the rough and dusty road, knowing that every step is a hazard to them, is a sad and moving experience. On the other hand, to see them walking away with feet protected by "ready sandals" is to lift up the heart with adoration to God, and admiration for His servants who, under Him, have made the wonderful change possible.

THE ABSENTEE

"But Thomas...was not with them when Jesus came" —
John 20:24

Christ came, but Thomas was not there
His word to hear, His love to share.
While others felt the warmth of His embrace,
He missed the beauty of the Master's face.

Doubt dulled the mind and closed the heart,
Which once had sworn to take the part
Of Christ against the world, whilst unbelief
Ate like a canker, adding to his grief.

All too often we are absent
When Jesus comes, and may lament
Our lack of strength in face of pain and death:
Had we been there, we too would feel His breath.

Why should we do ourselves this wrong?
Why weak? When He could make us strong
When Jesus comes to meet His own,
Let us be there, at prayer before His throne.

11

THE KINGDOM IS JOY

JOY IS AN ELUSIVE and unpredictable element in life. It does not come at the call of authority, nor is it manufactured by propitious circumstances. It appears when least expected and survives when all else seems lost. It is not in the happiness of the rescued but in the triumph of those who see defeat as a way of inner victory. It is not the happiness of those with great possessions, but the joy of those who are content with what they have, be it much or little. The early disciples were filled with joy in their periods of seemingly abject defeat. The Ascension robbed them of the visible presence on which they had relied since the earliest days of discipleship, but it gave them the supreme joy of a richer faith which required no outward sign (Luke 24:52,53). Even in the persecution which followed their proclamation of the Risen Christ, they were filled with joy (Acts 5: 41,42).

The Apostle Paul's clarion call was to a life expressing a joy undiminished by adversity; indeed his own testimony was that vicissitudes only prepared for later joy and enlarged life's capacity to receive it. His constant affirmation was that "the Kingdom of God is . . . joy in the Holy Ghost" (Romans 14:17). It is not surprising, therefore, that in spite of the use of such epithets as "kill-joy" and "dismal Jimmies" there has been a continuous stream of joyous influence wherever the Church has truly followed her Lord. The orphan has been sheltered, the sick cared for, the desolate uplifted and the lonely befriended.

The followers of St. Francis were called "the Jongleurs of God" — "God's gleemen," because their joy was as contagious as their service was beneficial. Most of the early hospitals were the outcome of Christian compassion, and the welfare of the underprivileged, as for instance the liberation of slaves, was the concern of men who had themselves found true liberty in Jesus Christ.

The care of the sick, so great a concern of our Lord, has ever been a priority in the service of His followers and the "Houses of Pity", though known in non-Christian lands as early as 260 BC., came into prominence as an outreach of the ministry of the Gospel. Basil the Great erected a *Ptochotropheion* or hospice in 370 A.D. for the relief of the sick and poor at Caesarea, and there is a tradition that the sick cared for included leprosy sufferers (J. Morrison Hobson, *Houses of Pity* p.3). Chrysostom, Augustine, and Benedict all sought to ally the preaching of the Gospel with the serving of the afflicted, and established their religious houses under this rule.

Spenser's *Faerie Queen* (Book 1 Canto X) published in 1589, reminds us of the loving attention given to the sick in mediaeval days:

> "Eftsoons unto an holy Hospitall,
>   That was foreby the way, she did him bring;
>   In which seven Bead-men, that had vowed all
>   Their life to service of High Heaven's King,
>   Did spend their days in doing godly things.
>   Their gates to all were open evermore,
>   That by the wearie way were travelling,
>   And one sate wayting ever them before,
>   To call in commers-by that needy were and pore."

Into that great tradition of selfless service have come those whose names we remember in the list of workers printed by The Leprosy Mission under the title *At His Feet,* an adjunct to the cycle of prayer, *Daily Remembrance.* To live in their homes and to watch them in their service is to catch the joy of those who have "vowed all their life to service of High Heaven's King." With them, also, we remember those other workers without whom their service would be impossible; dressers in the ulcer clinics, compounders in the dispensaries, orderlies and nurse-aides in the wards, technicians in the laboratories and paramedical workers in the villages. I have often thought it highly significant that when leprosy workers and their patients try to find a name for a new institution, they so often incorporate in the title a sense of joy: three of the best known examples are "Anandaban" — "The Forest of Joy," Kathmandu, Nepal; "Hay Ling Chau" — "The Isle of Happy Healing," Hong Kong, and "The Happy Mount Colony", Taiwan. Arising from this same experience of joy is the glad song which welcomes the visitors, encourages the staff and expresses the inner feelings of the patients. The languages will vary from centre to centre but the song will be one because its source is one.

It was my good fortune to spend a Christmas at Purulia in West Bengal, and the lasting impression is that of Joy. In the school, at the Church of the Good Samaritan, on the sports field, and in the processions round the compound, the groups of patients vied with each other in their singing and instrumental music. Bengali lyrics, translations of English and American carols, and folk songs from tribal areas were interspersed with items composed by the patients themselves and all mirrored the Christmas joy.

The hundred or so child patients sang for us, boys like Jitu, found begging by the superintendent in Asansol some months before while spending a weekend with friends. On the Sunday morning, after attending a Church Service, Mr. Askew was driving with his host through the bazaar when he stopped at a place where beggars usually congregated seeking alms. He had recognised one of the beggars as a villager from Simonpur, where the Purulia staff hold a leprosy clinic. As they talked together, another beggar came up, a boy about twelve. His outstretched hands were badly deformed and the fingers were already clawing; one foot was ulcerated and was crudely bandaged.

Questioning elicited the fact that Jitu was an orphan and was unaware that care and treatment were available. Mr. Askew asked the young lad to make his way to Purulia and promised that he would be received with kindness. Two days later, when Mr. and Mrs. Askew returned to Purulia, they found Jitu waiting under the banyan tree — a popular gathering place for would-be patients. When I saw him, Jitu was cleanly dressed and had a merry smile, both elements which are usually foreign to the begging line in the bazaar. The ulcerated foot was already healing and there was every prospect that physiotherapy would save his hands from further damage. Without that auspicious meeting in the Asansol street, Jitu's chances of a full life would have been poor indeed.

When I heard him joining in the hymn, "Everyone sing victory to Jesus", I knew that although I could not understand his Bengali song I could enter into his joy, the joy of a situation transformed by the love of One who said, "These things have I spoken unto you, that my joy might remain in you, and that your joy might be full." (John 15:11).

Happiness "happens", for it is based on circumstances, but joy "abides" for it is centred in a life and service which do not depend on changing circumstances. It was "for the joy that was set before Him" that He "endured the cross, despising the shame" and there is something of this "joy in the midst of suffering" that bursts through the corporate suffering endured by a host of leprosy victims; a joy that transcends their plight as much as the Saviour's triumphant cry arose above the agony of Calvary. It is the joy which Robert Louis Stevenson felt when he wrote, "The true realism, always and everywhere, is . . . to find out where joy resides, and give it a voice far beyond singing."

Jean Ingelow invites us to

" . . . take joy home,
And make a place in thy great heart for her,
And give her time to grow, and cherish her;
Then will she come, and oft will sing to thee,
When thou art working in the furrows; aye,
Or weeding in the sacred hour of dawn.
It is a comely fashion to be glad —
Joy is the grace we say to God."

EVEN SO SEND I YOU

"When I sent you without purse, and scrip, and shoes, lacked
ye anything? And they said, Nothing" — Luke 22:35

No scrip, no purse; And yet He sent them forth,
     A world to win.
A world that restless tossed as on a wave,
A world He left His Father's Home to save,
     From all its sin.

No purse of gold, but in each heart a key,
     To wealth unknown.
His was the power that made blind eyes to see,
Theirs was the word to make a people free,
     And Christ enthrone.

No scrip had they, but graven on each heart,
     A peerless Name.
In flaming letters as of fire it glowed.
Reminding them that all to Him they owed:
     He was their aim.

No scrip, no purse. Yet as He sent them forth,
     They feared no call.
For each within his heart, His Lord had crowned.
He was the Christ of God; in Him they found,
     Their all in all.

12

IN THE FOOTSTEPS OF WILLIAM CAREY

A BRIEF NOTICE in the *Calcutta Gazette* for November 14th 1793 announced the arrival of the good ship *Krön Princessa Maria* the previous week. On board was William Carey and India was to be his home until his death in 1834.

His desire was to help the people of India, a task which Carey called "the most arduous, honourable and important work that ever any of the sons of men were called to engage in." *(Farewell letter to his father, dated Jan. 17th, 1793).* The date of Carey's arrival was November 11th, 1793, the very same day that the French revolutionists tore down the Cross from Notre Dame and smashed it to pieces on the street below. The action of the French mob was more spectacular, but the arrival of Carey in India has been more productive for the world. The previous year, on May 31st 1792, Carey had made his impassioned appeal for the Church to enlarge its borders of thought and action. That sermon marked the beginning of the modern missionary movement. "Lengthen thy cords," ran his text, "and strengthen thy stakes." "Expect great things from God," said the cobbler turned preacher, "and attempt great things for God."

"If all the people had lifted up their voices and wept, as the children of Israel did at Bochim, I should not have wondered at the effect," remarked Dr. John Ryland after Carey's sermon, adding, "it would only have seemed proportionate to the cause, so clearly did Mr. Carey prove the criminality of our supineness in the cause of God!" The brother-ministers of Carey, who heard his sermon at the conference of the Northamptonshire Baptist Association held in the Friar Lane Chapel, Nottingham, did not weep, indeed most of them seemed eager to leave the Chapel the moment the service ended. As he saw the conference members departing, seemingly unmoved by his appeal, Carey seized the hand of Andrew Fuller and cried in an agonised voice: "Are we not going to do anything? Fuller, call them back, call them back! We dare not separate without doing anything." Something was done! The Baptist Missionary Society came into being with William Carey and John Thomas as its first missionaries. As I stood by William Carey's grave at Serampore, surrounded by the graves of his family and colleagues, I thought of "the lengthened cords and strengthened stakes!" In the College library an hour before, I had handled the precious volumes of Holy Scripture translated and prepared by Carey into Bengali, Oriya, Hindi, Marathi and Sanscrit. In the language of the crowds as well as the language of the scholars he had fulfilled his pledge "to give a New Testament to men who had never seen one before."

It was not only his Bibles, student text books and tracts which brought enlightenment. As a preacher and teacher, as a naturalist and agriculturist, as a man of conscience and a servant of compassion, William Carey opened doors of illumination and service. Suttee, the dreadful practice of widow-burning, which he himself had witnessed in 1799, was declared an illegal act as a result of his representations to the Governor-General. The murder of leprosy sufferers was another of the atrocities which he saw in the streets of Calcutta, and he established a "leper asylum" there where the victims of disease and ignorance might find sanctuary. The compassion Carey felt for the diseased, the exploited and the poor, passed over in his ministry to his converts, who were sent back into their own areas as ambassadors of the Kingdom of God. The burning of widows, the murder of the chronic sick and elderly unwanted, the abandoning of children and the frenzied suicide of Juggernaut devotees were attacked as being abhorrent to God and unworthy of His creatures.

One of Carey's Brahmin converts went back home to Allahabad — "city of god" where the sacred rivers of the Ganges and the Yamuna meet the legendary third river which gives the confluence the name *"Prayagraj"* — "King of Pilgrimages." Every winter crowds of pilgrims come from all parts of India to bathe at the point where the waters meet and every twelfth year, when the gathering of devotees is given the special name of *Kumbh Mela,* the pilgrims may be numbered by the million (in January 1956 the total number of pilgrims attending the mela was said to be $7\frac{1}{2}$ millions, making it the largest religious gathering in the world). Because of the special nature of the January Festival, Allahabad has always had more than its share of beggars, cripples and chronic sufferers seeking remembrance and generosity in alms from the pilgrims who hope to gain merit by their gifts.

It was this situation that led Carey's convert, in 1830, to receive leprosy beggars and others into a simple asylum on the outskirts of Allahabad. It was inconceivable for him to preach tidings of a God of Love to the crowds of pilgrims who thronged the riverside, and to do nothing to alleviate the suffering of the outcasts. In 1862 a new asylum was built on a better site a few miles east of the city by the District Charitable Association, superintended by missionaries of the American Presbyterian Church.

Comparable institutions for the care of the blind and the poor were also provided.

In 1875 further developments took place but when the Leper Act of 1898 was enforced, giving police the power to arrest and segregate leprosy beggars, the facilities at the Allahabad asylum proved inadequate and in 1904 The Mission to Lepers in India and the East as The Leprosy Mission was then named, was invited to take over and develop the work. Through the years the Allahabad Home and hospital at Naini has grown into a model leprosy centre catering for the needs of well over a thousand patients in spacious wards and well-equipped out-patient clinics.

Dr. Sam Higginbottom, an American agriculturist missionary professor, was among the earlier superintendents who guided the work at Naini and, more recently, the hospital has been under the leadership of Dr. J. J. Isaacs, ably supported by Mrs. Isaacs who is also a qualified doctor.

At Naini I saw the fruits of a work of which William Carey saw only the seed. The cords had, indeed, lengthened; from the little cobbler's shop at Hackleton and the chapel at Friar Lane, to the College at Serampore and the Printing Press in Calcutta; from the preaching stations by the Hoogli River to the leprosy hospital by the Ganges and the Tamuna Sangam.

Carey has still a word for us in our generation and it remains unaltered, for it comes direct from Isaiah, speaking as the prophet of God: "Lengthen thy cords . . . strengthen thy stakes . . . expect great things from God . . . attempt great things for God."